WHOSE BACKSIDE?

by

Rebecca Phillips-Bartlett

Minneapolis, Minnesota

Credits

Images are courtesy of Shutterstock.com. With thanks to Getty Images, Thinkstock Photo, and iStockphoto. Cover – Phillip Wittke, Artur Reinard, Naveen Kumar Gadhameedi. Recurring – Frogella, gambar_seru. 2–3 – Natalia Fedosova, Sanit Fuangnakhon. 4–5 – Mateo Juric, Nan Liu. 6–7 – Manoj Kumar Tuteja, MyImages - Micha, prapass, Sergey Uryadnikov, ClassicVector. 8–9 – Roger de la Harpe, walled fouad. 10–11 – A Periam Photography, Dolfilms, Hung Chung Chih, Jakub Krechowicz, alexcoolok. 12–13 – Felineus, slowmotiongli. 14–15 – Craig Lambert Photography, ericlefrancais, Erin Westgate, PHOTOOBJECT, TAW4. 16–17 – JacobLoyacano, Vladimir Turkenich. 18–19 – Alexey Seafarer, Deckar 007, LesPalenik, Sophia Granchinho, Amanita Silvicora. 20–21 – AndreAnita, Ondrej Prosicky. 22–23 – Brad Chapman, Fer Gregory, khlungcenter, Natalia Fedosova, tonyzhao120.

Bearport Publishing Company Product Development Team

Publisher: Jen Jenson; Director of Product Development: Spencer Brinker; Managing Editor: Allison Juda; Editor: Cole Nelson; Associate Editor: Naomi Reich; Associate Editor: Tiana Tran; Art Director: Colin O'Dea; Designer: Kim Jones; Designer: Kayla Eggert; Product Development Specialist: Owen Hamlin

Library of Congress Cataloging-in-Publication Data is available at www.loc.gov or upon request from the publisher.

ISBN: 979-8-89232-734-3 (hardcover)
ISBN: 979-8-89232-784-8 (paperback)
ISBN: 979-8-89232-821-0 (ebook)

For more information, write to Bearport Publishing, 5357 Penn Avenue South, Minneapolis, MN 55419.

CONTENTS

WHOSE BACKSIDE COULD THIS BE?

Different creatures use their backsides for different things. But can you guess an animal just from its rear end? Whose backside could that be lying in the grass?

What can a backside tell us about an animal?

It was a **CHEETAH'S** backside!

On the following pages, you will see photos of some behinds and three different animals. Look at the pictures and read the clues to guess whose backside is shown. Then, turn the page to find the answer.

A BIG BACKSIDE

Below is the first backside. What do you notice about it?

This behind is very big. Maybe it belongs to a large animal.

Take a closer look. There may be some poop stuck to this animal's tail.

Whose backside could it be? Choose which animal you think best fits this backside.
Hippo
Elephant
Rhino
Hippo . . . or hip-*poo*?

WHOSE BACKSIDE IS IT?

It is the **HIPPO'S** backside!

The hippo has a pretty smelly way of spreading its business. When a hippo poops, it uses its tail to fling its waste as far as possible. This helps the hippo mark its **territory** and warn others to back off.

A hippo has 36 teeth. When other animals are nearby, the hippo opens its mouth wide and shows off its huge teeth. This is meant to scare away other animals.

This animal only attacks with its teeth to **protect** its group.

Hippos eat mostly grass, leaves, and other plants.

A SUPER-STRIPY BACKSIDE

Here is another photo of an animal's backside. Whose could it be?

This rear end has white stripes.

The white stripes look like flickers of light. This could help **camouflage** the creature.

The striped pattern is easy to spot from up close.

Which of these animals might have a backside like this? Choose one.

WHOSE BACKSIDE IS IT?

It is the **OKAPI'S** backside!

Camouflage patterns help okapis live in their rainforest homes. Baby okapis, called calves, follow their mom's striped behinds through dark areas.

Zebras aren't the only ones with stripy behinds around here!

Okapis are **related** to giraffes. Like giraffes, these animals have long tongues. They use their tongues to grab leaves off tree branches.

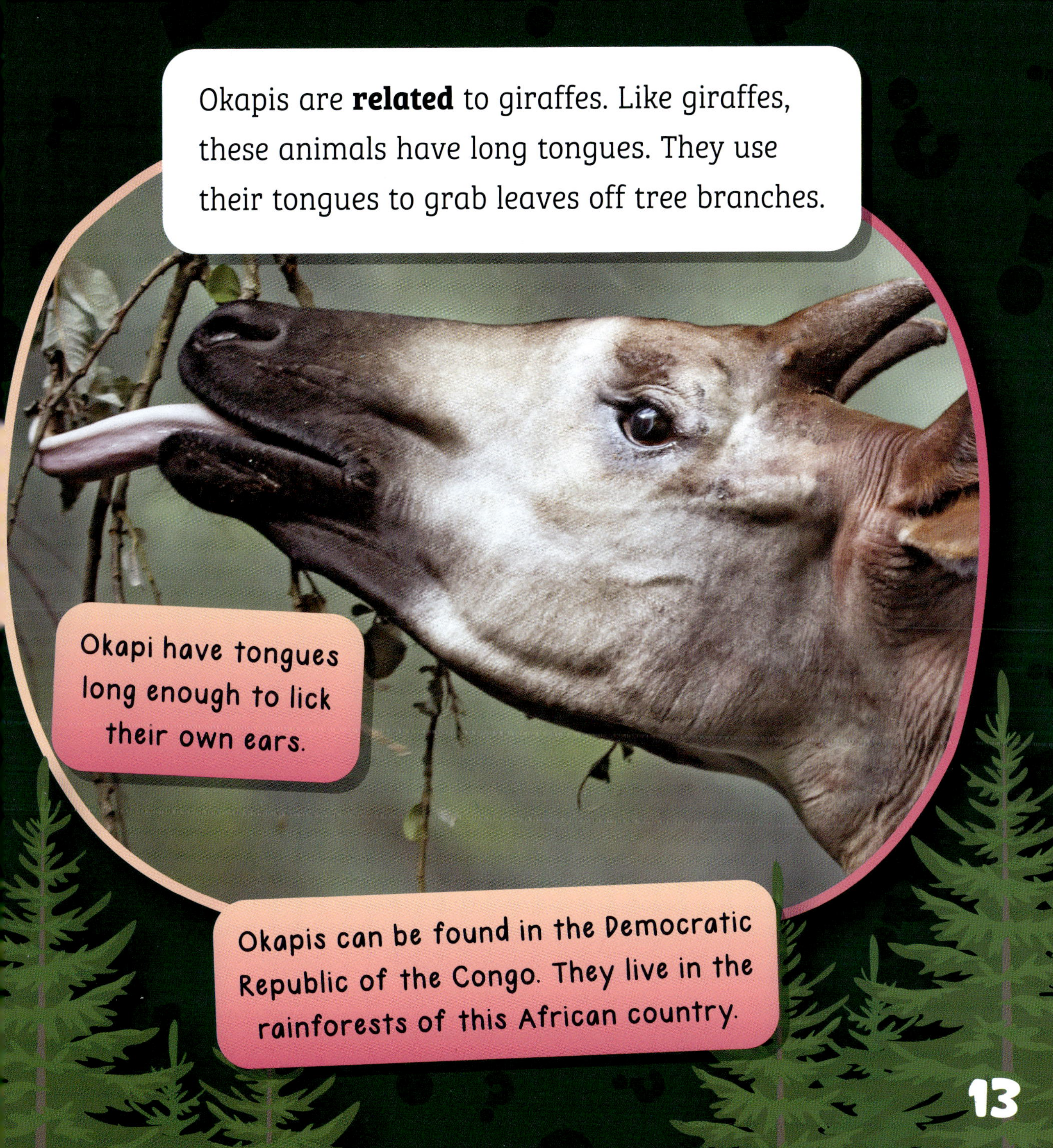

Okapi have tongues long enough to lick their own ears.

Okapis can be found in the Democratic Republic of the Congo. They live in the rainforests of this African country.

A PADDLE-SHAPED BACKSIDE

Here's another animal. . . . But wait, is that a tail?

This tail looks like it's underwater. It might help the animal float or move through the waves.

The tail is shaped like a paddle.

It looks like **algae** is growing on the tail. Algae often grows when there is a lot of sunlight.

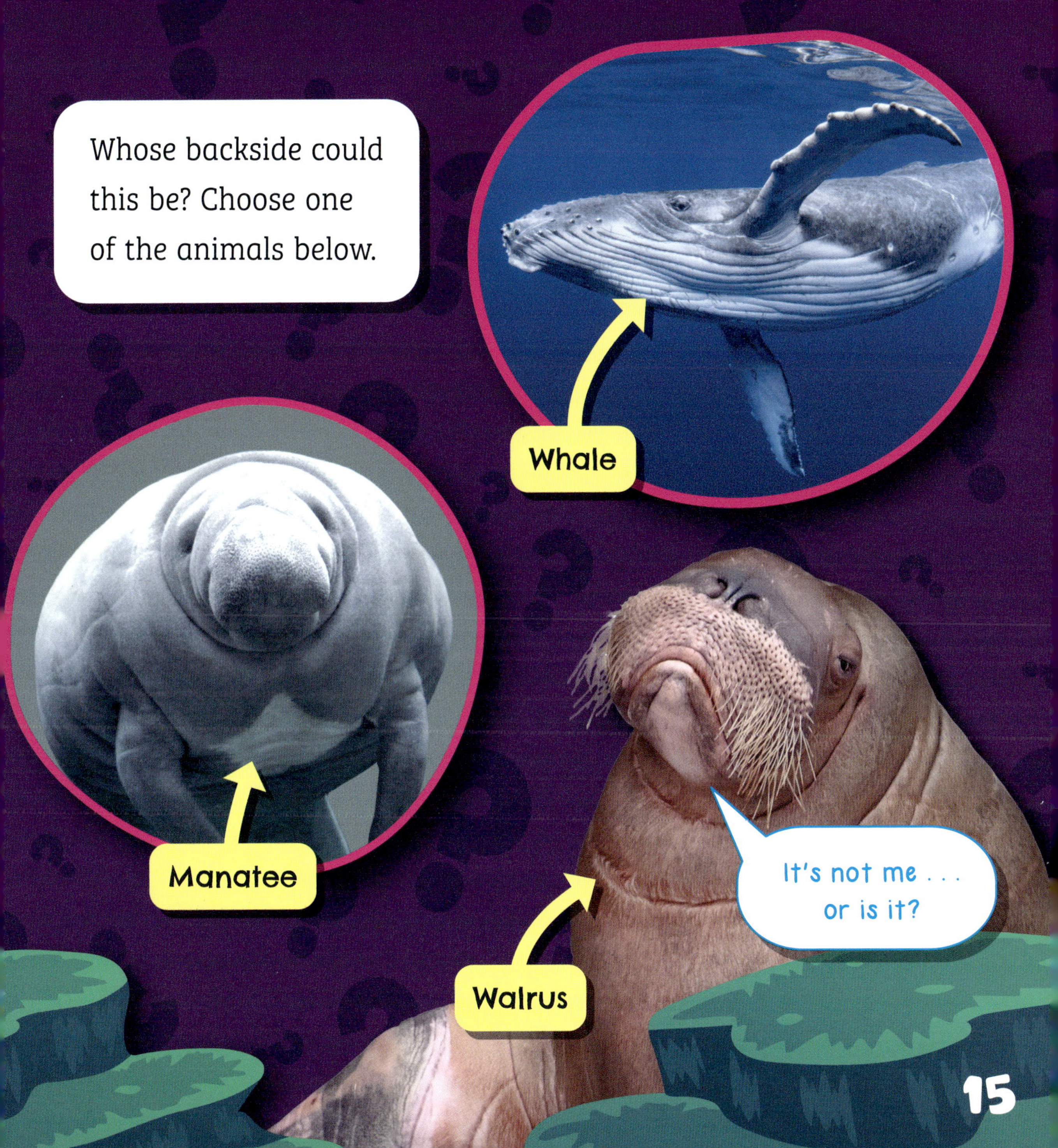
Whose backside could this be? Choose one of the animals below.
Whale
Manatee
Walrus
It's not me . . . or is it?

WHOSE BACKSIDE IS IT?

It is the **MANATEE'S** backside!

Wait until you find out what else my behind can do!

Most manatees are gray in color. But the algae growing on their tails makes them look green or brown.

Manatees are very strong swimmers. They use their tails to push themselves forward. These animals can swim as fast as 15 miles per hour (20 kph) for short periods of time.

Manatees can control their farts to float or sink in the water!

Manatees are often called sea cows. This is because they **graze** on underwater plants.

A BUSHY BACKSIDE

Brr! It looks like this animal might live in the Arctic. Whose backside could this be?

This animal's furry behind looks white. But is it actually white?

The animal's tail is very small. Can you see it?

Whose bushy bottom could this be? Make a choice from the following animals.

WHOSE BACKSIDE IS IT?

It is the **POLAR BEAR'S** backside!

Polar bear fur isn't really white. It's actually **hollow** and see-through. Light from the sun makes it appear white. And more surprising, a polar bear has black skin underneath its fur.

To stay warm, polar bears have another layer underneath their skin. This thick layer, called blubber, is made of fat. It's like wearing a winter coat all the time.

A small tail doesn't let much heat escape from the polar bear's big body.

Polar bears are the largest **carnivores** on Earth!

BONUS

BACKSIDE

A BRIGHT BEHIND!

Each firefly **species** has its own flashing pattern.

Many fireflies can make their backsides light up. These beetles use their lights to find **mates**. Bright bottoms also warn other animals to stay away.

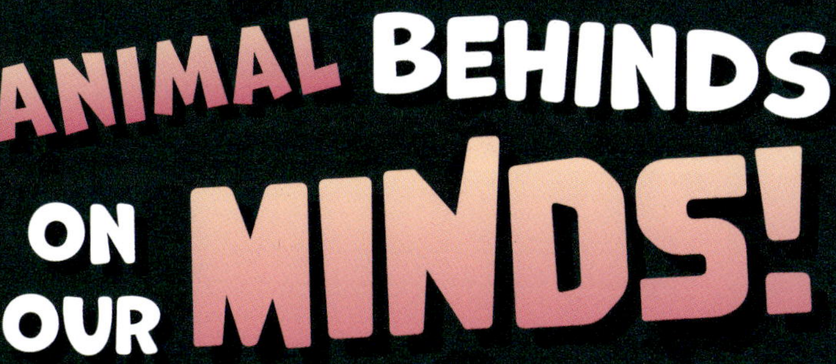

ANIMAL BEHINDS ON OUR MINDS!

There are so many kinds of animal backsides, from paddle-shaped to covered in fur. Backsides help creatures move from one place to another and stay safe as they are doing it. How does your backside help you?

GLOSSARY

algae a plantlike living thing that is often found in water

camouflage to hide by blending into the surroundings

carnivores animals that eat meat

graze to eat grass and other plants

hollow empty inside

mates partners that come together in order to have young

protect to keep from harm

related connected as members of the same family

species groups that animals are divided into

territory an area of land that belongs to an animal

INDEX